Chiavari It:
Travel Tips

Discover the most up-to-date and amazing places to sleep, eat, and shop in the Liguria region (Chiavari), along with essential information about the city

Hudson Miles

All rights reserved. No part of this publication may be reproduced, distributed, or transmitted in any form or by any means, including photocopying, recording, or other electronic or mechanical methods, without the prior written permission of the publisher, except in the case of brief quotations embodied in critical reviews and certain other noncommercial uses permitted by copyright law.

Copyright © (Hudson Miles) 2024

This pocket travel book which mainly focuses on **RECOMMENDATIONS** is a must-have when searching for the best places to stay, eat, and shop, along with their contact details. It also includes the city's affordable transport services and their phone numbers with essential information about the city and its Attractions.

Table Of Contents

Chiavari

Attractions

Leisure Activities

Practical Information

Transport Services

Accommodation

Restaurants

Shopping

Phrases and Slang Terms

Liguria Region

Visa

If you are not a citizen of a European Union (EU) or Schengen Area nation, you will usually need a visa to enter Italy. The reason and duration of your stay may necessitate a different visa.

Requirements may vary based on the type of visa (tourist, work, study, etc.). Generally, you'll need a completed application form, passport, passport-sized photos, travel itinerary, proof of accommodation, financial means, and, depending on the visa type, additional documents

scan the QR code above

You can also download the visa application form, fill it out, print it, and take it to the Visa Application Centre for submission.

Refer to the details of the Tourist Office in this guide for additional personal information.

Chiavari

On the Gulf of Tigullio, Chiavari is situated between the promontories of Portofino and Moneglia. Most people know it for being one of the busiest resorts on Liguria's coast, attracting many summer visitors because of its pebble beach and shoreline.

Away from the seaside, Chiavari is also known for its historic "carrugi," or alleyways, and for the fascinating fusion of its various architectural types.

If the beach is your reason for coming to Chiavari, you can find it on your own, but let us show you around the town's historic centre's highlights.

Designed by Leoni Cesario Marro between 1614 and 1633, Chiavari's most famous religious structure is the Shrine of Our Lady dell'Orto, a great place to start your tour. The Carmelite monks who oversaw its construction were relieved of their duties in 1797 following the proclamation of the Genoa Republic.

The first thing that draws attention is the pronaos (portico) by Luigi Poletti [1792–1869], which was modelled after the Pantheon in Rome. It consists of eight Corinthian columns composed of white marble. The building now seems to be a gigantic neoclassical structure, a testament to the architectural changes that have been sustained over time.

In the interior of the Shrine of Our Lady, there is an abundance of fine art, including the wooden group by Anton Maria Maragliano (1664–1739), the altar by Giovanni Ferradino (17th century), the chorus (17th century), and a fresco by Carlo Baratta that shows the "Translation of Our Lady".

Next, visit the Palace of Justice in the heart of the city. The palace, which was constructed in 1886 in the Tuscan-Gothic style, is located on the site of a mediaeval town whose ruins still contain a crenellated tower. Giuseppe Partini (1842–1895)

created this building in the style of central Italian architecture.
Neighbouring the Palace of Justice are the neoclassical White Palace and the municipal hall from the 19th century. Piazza Matteotti, or Carriage Square, is a prominent crossroads where the grounds of Villa Rocca dominate one side.

There are several distinct areas inside Villa Rocca Park, including the stunning orchid greenhouses, the bamboo forest, the rose garden, the area with cacti, the palm grove, and the area with oaks and conifers that are accentuated by ponds and fountains. The park is home to the "Tea Villa" and the "Temple of Music".

Directly beneath the grounds is Palazzo Rocca, a former home turned museum. Constructed in 1591–1657 by Bartolomeo Bianco, the building was later enlarged and dates to 1629.

Among the galleries and museums located in this palace are the Municipal Gallery, the Archaeological Museum of the Prehistory and Early History of Tigullio, and the Historical Museum of the Risorgimento.

Chiavaro Medieval and the Carrugi

The various historic buildings and "carrugi," the distinctive narrow streets from the Middle Ages, may be found in Chiavari's mediaeval old town.

Some of the most famous and fascinating of these include the 12th-century Palace of Black Portici. It has undergone numerous later rearrangements and features a gothic façade with four black pointed arches forming a large balcony.

It is also evident from strolling around the "carrugi" that Chiavari was a significant international port for many centuries, as you can recall from the hundreds of businesses that operated under the former arcades and were involved in a variety of activities.

Even while these traditional trades are still carried out in some hidden areas of Chiavari, the city's main boulevard, the "Caruggio Dritto," is home to a number of restaurants and well-known modern retailers

Approaching the coastal community of Chiavari, you will notice the striking Colonia Fara, a creation of engineer Camillo Nardi Greco in the 20th century. One prominent example of rationalist futurist architecture is this structure.

The structure appears asymmetrical in respect to the base because of its unusual design and the 43-metre-tall tower, which is located on the east side. It's obvious that the building is supposed to mimic an aeroplane.

Rupinaro's Saint James Church, formerly known as St Jacob de Arena, stands outside the fortified citadel and was probably built in the eighth or ninth century. Its striking 1938 façade is located in an architectural context reminiscent of the 17th century.

Statue of Garibaldi at a piazza
The church has a single nave with an altar by Francesco Schiaffino (1689-1765) and a baroque choir decorated with twelve religiously themed paintings by Giovanni Battista Carlone (1603-1684).

Another notable example of ecclesiastical architecture is the Church of St. John the Baptist in Chiavari. Built in 1181, it was extensively rebuilt between 1624 and 1631 by Andrea Vannone and Bartolomeo Rossi.

In 1935, Gaetano Moretti (1860-1939) provided funding for yet another repair of the façade.

Francesco Schiaffino's "Black Cross" and a few paintings by Domenico Piola, Orazio De Ferrari (1606–1657), and Domenico Fiasella are among the treasures crammed into three internal aisles.

Chiavari Cuisine

Ligurian specialties, such as "pesto," "trenette," and trofie (a kind of porridge made with chickpea flour), are reflected in Chiavari's cuisine. Not to mention the famous "thin capon" from Genoa and the "Pasqualina" cake. Another specialty that is exclusive to the region is "pansoti," which are ravioli stuffed with ricotta and herbs.

Bit Of History

The city's ancient beginnings, most likely from the eighth or seventh century BC, are attested to by the ruins of a necropolis found in the city centre. It was called "Tigullia" in the Roman era. The village was first mentioned as "Chiavari" in documents dated between 980 and 1031.

Genoa took on new lands, constructed a wall in 1168, erected a castle, and fought the Fieschi, the Counts of Lavagna. Together with the Malaspina, the Bobbio lords, these attempted in vain to seize possession of the Castle in the twelfth century.

During its time under Genoa, Chiavari had rapid urban and economic growth. As a result, it was given independence as a Municipality in 1242. Nonetheless, the Fieschi succeeded in regaining control of Chiavari's politics. They occupied it until 1332, when the settlement was recaptured by the Republic of Genoa, who then used it as the captaincy's headquarters for the Tigullio region.

In 1393, the Fieschi attempted one more time to seize the city. Chiavari thereafter coexisted with Genoa for decades until 1646, when it was granted town status.

In 1797, Napoleon ended the Republic's secular existence and combined it with the French Empire (1805–1814) and the Ligurian Republic (1797–1805).

The city functioned as the capital of the Apennines until the year of the Congress of Vienna's Restoration (1815), at which point it was taken over by the Kingdom of Sardinia (1815–1861). In 1861, Chiavari and Liguria were admitted to the Italian Kingdom.

What's Observable

Travelling southeast along the Ligurian coast, you will reach the town of Chiavari around five miles north-west of Sestri Levante and just four miles south of Zoagli.

This town is a true representation of Italian culture, unlike Rapallo, where the shoreline is neither the main draw or the main reason to visit.

With 28,000 residents, Chiavari is nearly as big as Rapallo and bigger than most of the other Riviera di Levante beach villages we've written about. The only thing separating it from the town next door, Lavagna, is the Entella River, albeit Chiavari is the more interesting of the two.

- Viale Enrico Millo

Not many people talk about Chiavari, especially when it comes to tourism, yet compared to most Ligurian villages, this one offers far more to see. Its largely grey gravel beach isn't exactly the most gorgeous seashore, but it's certainly not awful for an ultramodern, functional beach.

But away from the coast, Chiavari is a vibrant, bustling city with a sophisticated air that doesn't rely too heavily on tourists or its waterfront.

- Square Mazzini in Chiavari

It seems less conventionally Ligurian than most, with a blend of architectural styles and well-preserved structures that could be found in a city distant from the sea in Piedmont or Emilia Romagna. As it happens, Chiavari provides a welcome diversion from Rapallo for tourists visiting the Ligurian coast. Here, residents are more focused on their everyday lives than on entertaining guests.

Moreover, there are no credible signs that anyone in the town centre is thinking about tourism. Never undervalue the value of a little change of scenery—you won't find places like Chiavari through your travel agent.

A great place to start your walking tour of Chiavari and to get a feel for the town is via Viale Enrico Millo, where you can see some outstanding examples of immaculate late 19th- and early 20th-century Liberty style buildings.
These wide, palm-lined streets are perfect for strolling and are never crowded, even though they are not quite boulevards.

We decided to go to Chiavari on Sundays because of the great atmosphere and large crowds at the antiques and art market on those days.

It is well worth your time if you can fit this into your schedule. It usually happens on the second weekend of each month. If you enjoy people watching, this is the time and place to do so, especially with all those hand gestures and exaggerated mannerisms that make Italians so famous.

This is not your typical flea market (Mercato delle Pulci); this is a bonafide antique and art market (Mercato dell'Antiquariato). For example, it's significantly better than its equal in Lucca. Additionally, a decent assortment of interesting and well-made bric-a-brac is available, so you should be able to discover something small to take home.

Proceed up Via Martiri della Liberazione, where the market day stalls start just off Enrico Millo, even if it's not market day.

Here, the walkways eventually give way to a long expanse of historic porticoes on both sides of the road, evoking images of Bologna and several other Italian cities.

They bear witness to the rise of the new mercantile class in the later half of the fourteenth century and show the growth and importance of Chiavari during that time. The Chiavari porticoes have some beautifully preserved etched glass shop fronts from the Liberty period and beyond, but they lack the sculpted columns and magnificent arches of Bologna.

Pastry Copello's, Chiavari
Chiavari doesn't seem to be suffering economically because practically every area under the porticoes is filled with stylish boutiques, shops, gelaterie, and pasticcerie, many of which have kept their amazing old interiors that contribute to the sense of antiquity.

In Italy, there appears to be a direct relationship between the quality of a cafe's pastries and coffee and its interior design. The morning coffee ritual gains a wonderful element when one walks into one of these late 19th-century coffee shops, which sometimes have highly beautiful mirrors and marble fittings. This element may come from a sense of tradition and history.

Despite Covid, places like Chiavari also bear witness to the fact that Italians have not yet adopted the internet shopping habits of many other countries. Or perhaps the hubbub and bustle outside the stores has more to do with the fact that Italians enjoy getting together on the weekends to talk over coffee in the morning. Located in the portico at 164

Via Martiri, the Liberty-style Pasticceria Copello was founded in 1826 and is an excellent place to stop for coffee.

Chiavari's Giacomo Matteotti Square
As you follow Via Martiri farther, you will ultimately arrive at Piazza Mazzini, It is noteworthy that Chiavari was the place of birth for both Mazzini's and Garibaldi's fathers. The Palazzo di Giustizia, which sits behind Mazzini's statue, is ornamented in a mediaeval style, despite having been constructed in 1886. This is a nice piazza with a big outdoor market offering fruit, vegetables and cheese every day from early in the morning until midday.

Proceeding, Via Martiri empties into Piazza Giacomo Matteotti, which is much bigger than other piazzas along this coast since it is flatter here before the mountains rise. And then there's the great man himself, towering in the centre of the piazza, looking down Corso Garibaldi toward the ocean and the equally majestic statue of Christopher Columbus.

Every image in this collection of articles on the Riviera di Levante has a hint of the tropics, as you will see. There are palm trees everywhere, but nowhere is this more apparent than in Chiavari, which boasts the Parco Botanico di Palazzo Rocca, its own public gardens.

Botanical Park of Chiavari
This beach boasts an exceptional microclimate because the mountains completely block out any cold breezes from the northeast.

The Riviera di Levante's warm climate has long been one of its greatest attractions; on bright days in late winter and early spring, this is clearly evident. In comparison to the much colder Adriatic shoreline on the same latitude, where the environment is often too frigid even for olive trees, let alone palms, this is especially true.

La Brinca
Chiavari has one additional attraction for those who would like to cap off their journey to Ligurian with a magnificent dinner. The Trattoria La Brinca is located high in the hills six miles away in Ne. We have never been disappointed by La Brinca and

have always had wonderful experiences there. Despite its isolated location, we've seen people eating lunch there from as far away as Milan because it's that good. We've already mentioned that their pesto genovese is worth the trip.

Chiavari with kids

Discover the best places to visit in Chiavari with kids, family-friendly hotels, and other reasons why this town makes an excellent base for a Ligurian family holiday.
Chiavari, a gorgeous beach town in Liguria in the north of the country, is one of my favourite family-friendly travel spots in Italy.

Chiavari is well connected to Genoa, Milan, and Rome. It is located on the stunning Ligurian coast. Additionally, because of their extraordinary beauty, Portofino and the Cinque Terre are nearby and highly sought-after by both residents and foreign tourists.

Chiavari is the perfect temporary home for families looking for a small, local Italian coastal town that is close to the international tourist hotspot but also far enough away from it. Chiavari's kid-friendly atmosphere, beaches, flat promenade ideal for strollers with kid-friendly entertainment, and a

plethora of restaurants and cafes are sure to please families.
Some retailers and utilities that you may need for your kids are supermarkets and small-town shops.

Chiavari has ferries and trains, so you could just use it as a base to explore the area!
If my excitement about Chiavari as a destination for family vacations comes across, it's because I genuinely love this town!

- Why would you bring kids to Chiavari?

I suggest visiting Chiavari with your family if:

You're looking for an authentically native Italian beach village with first-rate tourism facilities.

You want a city with kid-friendly attractions and a flat promenade that's good for strollers for long summer evenings.

You want a neighbourhood where young kids can play together in the parks and playgrounds of the city.

Your family is looking for a handy starting location to catch boats to the Cinque Terre and Portofino (spring to early autumn only).

You like travelling by train and ferry to do your exploring.

Pesto is just the start of what you want to try when it comes to Ligurian cuisine!
The playground in Chiavari's inner city has a colourful slide.

How about taking the children to Chiavari?
Alternative choices are something you should consider if:

You want to go for a drive. Cars are possible here, although they are more of a hassle than a help because of parking and traffic problems, especially in the peak travel season.

If you're looking for wide, spacious, soft, sandy beaches, Chiavari contains more pebbles than sand.

You're looking for a place with lots of unspoiled beaches and scenic natural beauty. Chiavari is a built town by the sea, not a beach resort with few buildings and a "wild" vibe, despite its breathtaking stretch of shoreline

You're looking for a city with lots of kid-friendly English language programs and activities. Chiavari attracts more local than international tourism, as well as more European than American visitors, therefore activities like cooking lessons, etc., which are especially popular with US travellers, are consequently less common there than elsewhere.

In Chiavari, how long may a family stay?
How much time do you have left? All kidding aside, Chiavari is a nearby town where you could easily spend a whole summer having fun!
But if you would like to incorporate it in your itinerary for Italy, I would recommend staying in Chiavari for two or three nights. I would recommend staying in Chiavari for two nights with the kids if you are using it as a base to explore Cinque Terre or Portofino.

If you stay in Chiavari for two nights, you can take a ferry to Portofino or the Cinque Terre, tour the

town, and perhaps even visit one of the nearby towns, like Santa Margherita or Sestri Levante.
If you stay three nights, you can see Chiavari town and go on day tours to Cinque Terre and Portofino.

If you extend your stay beyond three nights, you'll have more time to explore the city and take the rail to many other surrounding locations.
and even Genoa!

In Chiavari, where may families stay?
Families visiting Chiavari should stay in the city centre, which is close to the sea and promenade.
We stayed at the lovely, immaculate three-star Hotel Santa Maria, which was perfect for our family.

Our hotel was spacious and had a sea view. It was quite hot when we arrived in Chiavari, so we were really grateful for the strong air conditioning. The breakfast was fantastic, including focaccia and other regional specialties in addition to classic Italian dishes.

From the station and the centre, it takes 7 to 10 minutes on foot to get to the hotel.

Even closer to the centre are these other stunning hotels:
Hotel Stella del Mare is a lovely family hotel in the centre of Chiavari that offers special services for small visitors, like kid-friendly meals and high chairs.

The four-star Hotel Monte Rosa has family rooms, a restaurant, and a swimming pool. The hotel may also help arrange for a cooking class in nearby Sestri Levante.

Convenient three-star Hotel dell'Orto in Chiavari, close to the promenade, the beach, and the station. Nice family rooms.

Check more hotel recommendations in the ending page of this guide

The best family-friendly activities in Chiavari
On my list of the best family-friendly things to do in Chiavari, the most popular day trips come first. Then, we'll talk about the best things to do in the city!

- Take a ferry to San Fruttuoso.

San Fruttuoso is a stunning monastery situated on a rocky cove, around an hour's ferry ride from Chiavari. The monastery is beautiful, but the main draw in the summer is swimming in the clean waters of the bay.

There are two main swimming areas in San Fruttuoso:

The majority of visitors gather just in front of the Abbey.

Five minutes' walk from the abbey brings you to a little cove with another small pebbly beach (but older kids would be better off because of the bumpy and steep approach).

In both cases, the water is clear enough for snorkelling. You should pack sandals, water shoes, and snorkelling gear because the beach is constructed of pebbles and the water is crystal clear!

I heartily recommend San Fruttuoso to families with older children who are happy to spend a few hours enjoying the water, despite its meagre services (a cafe, a small restaurant, and a place to rent beach chairs) Since the entire area is not wheelchair accessible, you should leave the stroller at home if you are visiting with a little child.

Knowing that the beaches and abbey are conveniently close to the boat stop makes sense. Bring all of your beach gear and wear water shoes because it's all rocks and large stones! The easiest approach to avoid the crowd at San Fruttuoso is to arrive here with the first ferry of the day, as it gets very packed. You can combine this excursion with a trip to Portofino.

- Take a ferry to Portofino.

Portofino is a gem, a place so beautiful it deserves all of its renown. Portofino is a little town that grew up around a marina and is situated in a gorgeous cove. A magnificent mediaeval castle towers over the marina.

With its restaurants, yachts, and private villas, Portofino is an upscale resort that doesn't have anything for youngsters to do.

But because it's so beautiful, it's worth stopping by. One of the most beautiful places in all of Italy, in my opinion, is Portofino.

With the children, we went to San Fruttuoso, where we went swimming, rode the ferry to Portofino, ascended the fortress, had lunch, and returned to Chiavari.

I wholeheartedly recommend everyone to enjoy this amazing day.

It's important to note that Portofino lacks kid-friendly attractions and playgrounds. If you are bringing small ones along, think of this as a day for them to explore with you rather than a day for them.

Without a stroller, you can climb the castle on foot. Hold hands if you bring small children into the castle grounds; some drops are safe for larger kids but may be hazardous for smaller ones.

It's preferable to know that while taking a ferry, families must move to the front of the line to board first. If they are unable to see you, show them the children, and they will bring you forward.

- Take a ferry to Cinque Terre Monterosso.

The best place to experience the Cinque Terre by boat is to stay in the towns of Cinque Terre or

Levanto, which are closer to the well-known five towns than Chiavari.
However, departing from Chiavari is also a smart move!
After taking the local ferries and rail to Monterosso, you can choose to either explore the town or take the ferry back to Chiavari.

- Go to the beach

Chiavari is a seaside town with a long stretch of beach clubs along the shore. Thus, taking your kids to the beach should be among your Chiavari activities!

Beautiful, clear water can be found in this location, and wave breakers have been added in some places to help protect small children.
The beach is made up of pebbles and dark sand, like most of this part of Liguria, so bring water shoes if you're not used to very soft sand!

- Chiavari Beach Club features wave breakers.

Some beach clubs in Chiavari that you might enjoy are:

Il Gabbiano can be booked online! Via Preli, 19, 16043 Chiavari GE, Italy

Bagni Ciccio: Corso Valparaiso; 16043 Chiavari GE, Italy

Tito Groppo Viale, Bagni Giardini, 2, 16043 Chiavari GE, Italy: This location, which was in front of our hotel and a little out from the centre, has beach chairs and umbrellas, sports fields, and a foosball table. It seemed to be quite well-liked by families. This beach welcomes dogs.

Even though Google Maps shows that there is a free beach close to Bagni Giardini, we were only able to locate an unattractive tiny stretch of shore with a difficult-to-access ocean and an abandoned water park in July. Yes, it's obvious that we were disappointed! The beach clubs are still great, though.
Chiavari's beaches are best visited in June through September.

- Check out the playground by the water's edge.

A straightforward yet enjoyable beach playground is situated close to Chiavari's pier.

There are climbing frames and a large rope structure for kids on the playground. It's a beautiful site with plenty of kids from the area, but be careful because it may become rather hot during the summer!

- Enjoy the Chiavari promenade.

Chiavari has a fantastic promenade with beach clubs on one side and eateries, cafes, hotels, and other businesses on the other.
Some places come to life on summer nights with cute kid's playthings like a trampoline and rides similar to a carousel.

After nightfall, the Chiavari seashore features a fantastic fountain with light games that are entertaining to watch!
It's good to know that Chiavari's promenade is home to an aircraft! It is owned by the Coast Guard and is quite amazing to see even for small children.

- View the playgrounds in Chiavari.

Apart from the beach playground described before, there's a great playground at Viale Enrico Millo, 16043 Chiavari GE, Italy, which also has a tiny zipline. There are lots of kids from the neighbourhood there.

Playgrounds can be found along the seafront at Piazza Roma and Corso Valparaiso (the area surrounding Via dei Velieri).

- Where can families eat in Chiavari?

Though some of these places are new to me, This list is based on my personal experiences there!

Lunch and dinner:
Vino e Cucina dal 1999: Delicious food is served at this restaurant. They might not seem family-friendly at first because of the design and plenty of wine bottles, but they're actually very kid-friendly!
It's not extravagant, but the food is excellent and well presented; they have some delectable seafood and shellfish sampling, such trofie al pesto, for the neighbourhood. On the posher end of the meal presentation range (my kids thought it was "very fancy").

Boccon Divino Fisherman's Restaurant, Via Bighetti, 107, 16043 Chiavari GE, Italy
Reputably good for Ligurian cuisine and something of an institution in Chiavari, Enoteca Defilla 16043 Corso Giuseppe Garibaldi, 4,
PIZZA M'AMA is located at Corso Valparaiso, 150, 16043 Chiavari GE, Italy.

Meals delivered and snacks:
The greatest focaccia in Chiavari may be found at Panificio Luca, Corso Montevideo, 21, 16043 Chiavari GE, Italy.
The greatest gelato may be found at Cremeria Spinola, Corso Valparaiso, 118.
A deli and takeout restaurant called Gastronomia Garibaldi can be found in 6/10 Via Mongiardini, 16043 Chiavari GE, Italy.

Best Aperitif in Chiavari:
Casa Gotuzzo, located at 20 Piazza Davide Gagliardo, 16043 Chiavari GE, Italy Nadu, serves aperitivo cuisine with chicken nuggets and is a laid-back, kid-friendly restaurant.

- How to get the children to Portofino from Chiavari

As said before, bringing kids from Chiavari to Portofino is a rather easy experience. However, keep the following in mind:
There isn't a ferry every day. Depending on the season, there might be a direct ferry most days or just a few.

The boat takes around minutes to get to from Chiavari by rail (we've done it, so it's not at all troublesome), but if it's not running on the day you visit, you will have to catch it from Rapallo. The dates are available on the ferry's website, https://traghettiportofino.it/linee-gite/.

Portofino is therefore not a place for kids. It's a beautiful place with excellent views and food options, but it's not the best place for younger kids who would prefer a playground or other amusement options. Older kids who like people watching on the luxurious yacht, on the other hand, might be a better fit.
If your kids are small, you may want to combine it with a kid-friendly activity like a trip to the nearby beach in Santa Margherita or some beach time in Chiavari.

- Marina Portofino

We found that the boat lines move rapidly, despite the fact that they can be frightening. The fact that they advanced us to the front of the line due to the kids was a really nice touch!
How to get from Chiavari to Cinque Terre with kids Chiavari is located north of the Cinque Terre, and it is connected to the area by frequent ferry services like the "Golfo del Tigullio."

However, docking locations for boats from Chiavari to Monterosso are restricted due to regulations regarding access to the Cinque Terre Gulf. Although Monterosso is the most family-friendly village in the Cinque Terre, it's still a good idea to be aware of your alternatives, particularly if you plan to go trekking.

One could:
Use the ferry line's journey to your advantage to visit the Cinque Terre districts from the water and spend four hours at Monterosso.
Go on a tour, spend four hours at Monterosso (the parks and beach will appeal to the youngsters), or use Monterosso as a jumping-off point to catch the train to another town to see more of the area.

It might seem like a last-minute option, but it's completely possible—the train from Cinque Terre town only takes a few minutes.

- How to go to Chiavari

The best way to go to Chiavari is by train.
By direct train (quite convenient!) to Chiavari from Rome. or Genoa, La Spezia, Milan, and other handy locations.
I hope you were inspired to visit Chiavari by our fun family-friendly tips!

Extra Exploration in Chiavari

The main areas of Chiavari include the marina, the seashore, and the old centre. While exploring the city, make a note of the sights that most intrigue you. Below are a handful of them:

- Borgolungo Chiavari

Borgolungo, Chiavari's old centre, features antique stores, mediaeval arcades, and characteristic carruggi from Ligurian culture.
The main boulevard, known to the locals as "Caruggio dritto," is where the social scene of Chiavari is located. This busy area is home to the most well-known cafes and premium stores.
To spend the afternoon shopping and meeting new people, all you need is a little.

- Marina Chiavari Porto di Chiavari

The harbour of Chiavari is one of Italy's most beautiful marinas. This port has undoubtedly become a symbol of the Mediterranean due to its advantageous placement close to well-known tourist destinations like Portofino and the Cinque Terre. But also regions beyond Liguria, such as Tuscany, Sardinia, and France, particularly Corsica and the French Riviera.

More than 550 boats are stored at this major facility, and there are another 151 in West Calata. Additionally, it offers access to all of the most recent websites for boating services.

Beyond being a place for recreation, Chiavari's harbour is an integral part of the city's urban environment and the second-biggest focus of social and commercial activity in the city, after the historic centre.

When in Chiavari, take a leisurely stroll along Corso Valparaiso, a 2-mile promenade dotted with restaurants, pizzerias, ice cream parlours, parks, and playgrounds for young visitors.

- Chiavari Castle

The ruins of the historic Castle of Chiavari, one of Tigullio's oldest castles, are all that are left.
Today, remnants of the city wall, the fortified parade field, and the Keep with its two water cisterns are all evident.

It is genuinely closed to the public, as this Chiavari sign is situated on private property.

- Our Lady of the Garden-focused basilica cathedral

The origin of the Cathedral of Our Lady of the Garden is the small chapel dedicated to the Virgin Mary that was abandoned in a garden, or "kitchen garden," in the twelfth century. There are legends of a healing spring with mystical abilities that appeared in the garden.

The growing veneration for this holy site led to the expansion of the shrine to build a church in the 14th century, and it was elevated to the status of a cathedral in 1616.

The magnificent architecture of the cathedral is a tasteful blend of Gothic and Ligurian design. The cathedral's calm aura is enhanced by the lovely landscape that surrounds it.

The stunning murals that cover its tall walls and domed roof will catch your eye right away, as do the exquisite stained-glass windows that flood the interior with a kaleidoscope of refracted light.

The impressive high altar is a wonder in and of itself, with its mesmerising gold-leafed wooden statue of Our Lady of the Garden. Another notable work of art that has been preserved inside the cathedral is the revered 14th-century Fasolo Crucifix, which is highly regarded by the city's residents.

- Park at Villa Rocca Villa-rocca-chiavari.

Enjoy the peace and quiet of Villa Rocca Park, a verdant sanctuary tucked away in the quaint Ligurian village of Chiavari. This magical botanical park, which boasts a vast variety of flora and a serene atmosphere, is open to both tourists and locals looking to escape the daily grind and enjoy the soothing benefits of nature.

Villa Rocca Park was established by the Rocca family, who came back from Argentina intending to recreate various natural environments from around the globe.

One of the most outstanding features of Villa Rocca Park is its amazing array of flora, which includes various succulents and rare varieties of trees.

This beautiful park is a refuge for outdoor enthusiasts as well as an art gallery. A wide range of sculptures that highlight the natural beauty of the area and pique visitors' curiosity are scattered across the verdant landscape.

For those seeking a getaway from the daily grind, Villa Rocca Park, one of Chiavari's most well-liked attractions, is a must-visit spot.

- Rapallo Palafitte

Savour the wealth of the lively town of Chiavari, located on the Italian Riviera. The city is surrounded by an amazing coastline with several beautiful beaches that are washed by the gentle waves of the Ligurian Sea. The beaches are easily accessible and often lined with busy enterprises, providing a calm respite for both locals and tourists.

Shared between Chiavari and Sestri Levante, this area of Liguria boasts the highest percentage of undeveloped beaches.

Nearly all of the city beaches are located on the sea promenade west of the marina, close to the city centre.

There are also beaches that are disability accessible and beaches with spaces set aside for dogs.

Additionally, from Chiavari, you can take in a change of scenery by visiting one of the numerous breathtaking beaches nearby:

- Lavagna Beach

Lavagna Beach is a long stretch of wide sand that is ideally located near the city of Chiavari. It gives beachgoers plenty of room to spread out their towels and soak up the Mediterranean sun.

Its calm seas and friendly ambiance make it the ideal destination for those travelling alone, with friends, or in a group.

- Zoagli Beach

To truly appreciate the serene beauty of Zoagli beach, walk a bit further. This tiny pebble beach offers breathtaking views of the turquoise sea surrounded by verdant hills of Ligurian beauty. Because it offers a tranquil experience away from the bustling crowds of the main beaches, locals adore it.

- Mouth of the Entella River

Adventure seekers can have a totally unique beach experience at the beach near the mouth of the Entella River. Its location on the river estuary makes it a popular destination for water sports like sailing, kitesurfing, and surfing, adding a thrilling element to the otherwise tranquil beach.

- Bay of Silence

A short drive from Chiavari is the quaint Baia del Silenzio in the nearby town of Sestri Levante. This beach is well-known for its picture-perfect surroundings and views. Encircled by pastel-coloured cottages, this charming crescent-shaped bay gives the authentic Ligurian Riviera experience.

Tourist Office: Tourist information centre in Chiavari, Italy

Location: Via Cittadella, 1, 16043 Chiavari GE, Italy
Phone Number: +39 0185 365400

Attractions

Below are more Attractions in the city, both popular and lesser-known ones. Visit any of them, depending on your preference.

- Palazzo Rocca:
  - Location: Piazza Giacomo Matteotti, 2

An art museum housed in Palazzo Rocca, showcasing cultural artefacts and artworks, providing insight into Chiavari's rich history and artistic heritage.

- Fontana con giochi di luce:
  - Location: Unnamed Road, 16043

A fountain with light displays, offering an enchanting sight and adding charm to Chiavari's ambiance, attracting visitors with its mesmerising features.

- Fontana 8 marzo:
  - Location: Corso Valparaiso, 50

The "8 marzo" fountain on Corso Valparaiso, serving as a landmark and gathering spot, contributing to the scenic beauty of Chiavari's streetscape.

- Promontorio di Chiavari con vista Gruppo del Sale:
  - Location: Chiavari, Metropolitan City of Genoa, Italy

The Chiavari Promontory offers panoramic views of the Gruppo del Sale mountains, providing a picturesque backdrop for visitors exploring the area.

- Piazza Mazzini:
  - Location: Piazza Mazzini, 7

Piazza Mazzini, a central square in Chiavari, surrounded by historic buildings and bustling with activity, serving as a focal point for locals and tourists alike.

- Mercato dell'antiquariato di Chiavari:
  - Location: Via Martiri della Liberazione

The antique market of Chiavari on Via Martiri della Liberazione, offering a treasure trove of vintage finds and collectibles for enthusiasts and collectors.

- Spiaggia libera:

- Location: Viale Tito Groppo, 2

Spiaggia Libera, a free beach along Viale Tito Groppo, providing a relaxing seaside retreat for locals and visitors to enjoy the sun and sea.

- PALAZZO GHIO:
  - Location: Via S. Giovanni, 1

Palazzo Ghio, a historic building on Via S. Giovanni, showcasing architectural beauty and cultural significance, offering glimpses into Chiavari's past.

- Cattedrale Basilica Santuario di Nostra Signora dell'Orto:
  - Location: Piazza Nostra Signora dell'Orto, 5

The Cathedral Basilica Sanctuary of Our Lady of the Orchard, a religious landmark in Chiavari, known for its architectural grandeur and spiritual significance.

- Tempietto neopompeiano:
  - Location: Parco di Villa Rocca, Piazza Giacomo Matteotti, 10

The Neo-Pompeian Temple in Villa Rocca Park, a unique architectural gem inspired by ancient Pompeian design, offering a serene retreat for visitors.

- SPAZIO CASONI:

- Location: Via Bighetti, 73

Spazio Casoni, a cultural space on Via Bighetti, hosting exhibitions and events, promoting artistic expression and creativity within the Chiavari community.

- Archaeological Museum of Chiavari:
  - Location: Via Costaguta, 4

The Archaeological Museum of Chiavari, home to artefacts from the Etruscan era, provides insights into the region's ancient civilizations and cultural heritage.

- Castello Di Chiavari:
  - Location: Salita Castello, 1

Chiavari Castle, a mediaeval fortress on Salita Castello, offers a glimpse into the town's military history and provides panoramic views of the surrounding landscape.

- Piazza dei pescatori punto panoramico:
  - Location: Chiavari, Metropolitan City of Genoa, Italy

Piazza dei Pescatori Panoramic Point, offering stunning views of Chiavari's coastline and bustling harbour, capturing the essence of maritime life in the region.

- Ponte della Maddalena Lavagna Chiavari:
  - Location: Via Ponte della Maddalena

The Ponte della Maddalena Bridge connects Lavagna e Chiavari, an architectural marvel spanning the river, offering a scenic route for travellers and locals alike.

- Tigullio Beach:
  - Location: Sant'Andrea di Rovereto, Metropolitan City of Genoa, Italy

Tigullio Beach in Sant'Andrea di Rovereto, a picturesque coastal stretch with golden sands and clear waters, perfect for sunbathing and swimming.

- Spiaggia Naturista:
  - Location: Chiavari, Metropolitan City of Genoa, Italy

Naturist Beach in Chiavari, offering a secluded and clothing-optional environment for those seeking a more liberating beach experience.

- Piaggio P 166 Guardia Costiera:
  - Location: Chiavari, Metropolitan City of Genoa, Italy

Piaggio P166 Guardia Costiera, a historic aircraft displayed in Chiavari, symbolising the town's connection to maritime and aviation history.

- Passeggiata di Chiavari:
  - Location: Corso Valparaiso, 86

The Passeggiata di Chiavari along Corso Valparaiso, a scenic promenade lined with shops, cafes, and gardens, ideal for leisurely strolls and people-watching.

- Museo Marinaro "Tommasino - Andreatta":
  - Location: Via Parma, 34

The Tommasino - Andreatta Maritime Museum on Via Parma, showcasing Chiavari's seafaring heritage through exhibits and artefacts, currently on renovations.

Leisure Activities

Below are activities to get involved in, suggestions on day trips and excursions, Embark on any of these activities to enhance your travel experience.

- Ligurian Cooking Classes: Immerse yourself in the flavours of Ligurian cuisine with hands-on cooking classes led by local chefs. Learn to prepare traditional dishes using fresh, local ingredients.

- Genoa Private Tour to Chiavari: Explore the historical town of Chiavari with a private tour from Genoa. Discover its charming streets, historical landmarks, and cultural treasures with a knowledgeable guide.

- Magnificent Tigullio - Gourmet and Historical Tour in Chiavari: Indulge in a gourmet journey through Chiavari, sampling delicious local delicacies while learning about the town's rich history and cultural heritage.

- Dining Experience at a Local's Home in Chiavari with Show Cooking: Experience authentic Ligurian hospitality with a dining experience at a local's home in Chiavari. Enjoy a delicious meal prepared by your host, complete with a show cooking demonstration.

- Andrea Boat Charter Portofino: Sail the stunning waters of Portofino with Andrea Boat Charter. Enjoy a customizable day trip, exploring hidden coves, picturesque villages, and breathtaking coastal views.

- Snorkel Tour in Paraggi Bay: Dive into the crystal-clear waters of Paraggi Bay on a snorkelling tour. Explore vibrant marine life and colourful underwater landscapes in this scenic coastal area.

- Ligurian Sea Day Sailing Trip by Set Sail Tours/Lavagna, Italy: Set sail on a day trip along the Ligurian Sea with Set Sail Tours. Relax onboard a sailing yacht as you cruise past scenic coastal vistas and enjoy optional stops for swimming and sunbathing.

- Sunset Cinque Terre Boat Tour with a Traditional Ligurian Gozzo from Monterosso: Experience the magic of a sunset boat tour along the Cinque Terre coastline. Sail aboard a traditional Ligurian gozzo from Monterosso, soaking in panoramic views of the rugged cliffs and colourful villages.

- Boat Rental in Portofino and Tigullio Gulf: Explore the stunning Portofino and Tigullio Gulf at your own pace with a boat rental. Enjoy the freedom to navigate the pristine waters and discover hidden coves and secluded beaches.

- Cinque Terre Sunset Tour: Witness the beauty of the Cinque Terre region at sunset on a guided tour. Capture stunning coastal views as the sun dips below the horizon, painting the sky with vibrant hues.

When travelling, it's advisable to book your tours in advance if interested. Consider using Viator for great deals. Scan the QR code to book online.

Travel Advice for Italy

Nobody likes to appear foolish
One of the most unpleasant experiences I've had while travelling was being warned by the police for eating ice cream in Piazza San Marco, Venice. simply because I had been so preoccupied with figuring out what to do in Venice.

Pack and Plan: Adapters, toiletries, travel documents, layers of clothing for variable weather, comfy walking shoes, and versatile pieces of clothing are essentials for any trip to Italy. It's crucial to travel light and refrain from overloading, choosing things that are both neutral and adaptable.

Packing can be made easier by researching the weather in advance and making clothing plans appropriately. It can be more convenient to travel with light clothing, a few jewellery items, and a roomy travel backpack or fanny pack. You can also prevent additional expenses by weighing your suitcase in advance and packing bulkier things for the airline.

General Info
Emergency Numbers: - Press 112 for assistance in all situations.
113 (thefts, accidents, and issues with the police).
- Fire Department: 115 (for weather-related issues and fire situations).
- Emergency Medical Care: 118 (for life-threatening illnesses or rescues from caves or mountains).
- 803.116 for Roadside Assistance (ACI).

Dial the international code +39 and then the number to make an Italian phone call.
- Dial 00, then the international code and number, to place an international call from Italy.
It is advised to get an Italian SIM card in order to communicate more affordably.

Budget Travel in Italy: Take low-cost airlines into smaller airports; take into account other modes of transportation, like high-speed trains connecting major cities.

To balance weather, costs, and to avoid the busiest times of the year, travel in May, June, September, and October, the shoulder seasons.

Using Public Transportation vs. Hiring a Car: Utilising public transportation is a more economical way to visit cities. Consider multi-day travel passes and buy your high-speed rail tickets in advance to save money.

Budget-Friendly Dining: Check out trattorias' fixed-price lunch menus for inexpensive lunch options.

Order your espresso at the bar to avoid additional service charges.

Fashion: Steer clear of the usual tourist outfit of sandals and white socks. Rather, dress tastefully and comfortably. **Cultural tip**: Cappuccinos are morning drinks; "caffe latte" is milk; and "Caffè shakerato" is iced coffee.

Avoid Getting a Cappuccino after 11am
It seems to interfere with your ability to digest.

Restaurant Hours: After lunch, restaurants close and reopen for dinner. However, bars and street food are open throughout the closures.

Electricity: Your electronics should include converters; use a two-pin European plug. **Shop and Service Hours**: In smaller cities and rural areas, especially, expect closures between 1 and 4 p.m.

City-Specific Advice: Pizza tastes peculiar to a city include "Pepperoni" (red peppers, not salami) and steer clear of Hawaiian pizza. Ask for the bill after lunch and be ready to have a long conversation.

Language: Acquire a few simple Italian expressions. It's possible that not everyone speaks English outside of tourist destinations.

Bathroom: Because bidets are so common in Italy, be conscious of their hygiene customs.

Savings Advice for Transportation:
ATM withdrawals can be made in Italian money if desired. When an ATM offers you the option to pay with your own money, it's a cunning ploy that leads to many travellers overspending. To save money and obtain the greatest deals, always opt to pay in the local currency, in this example, the euro.

Travel with budget airlines like **Vueling, EasyJet, Ryanair, or WizzAir.**

- Think about entering a city by land or travelling between cities on fast trains. As you go, buy tickets because train passes might not be the best deal. Examine point-to-point tickets and think about using the bus for some connections.

Local Transportation: - An extensive rail network connecting important Italian cities is maintained by **Trenitalia and Italo**.

- Areas not serviced by trains are covered by buses, while long-distance coaches are run by private companies like Flixbus.
- Coastal areas and islands are connected by ferries.

Driving in Italy: - If you're travelling through rural areas, renting a vehicle, motorcycle, or Vespa gives you more freedom.
- Roads are categorised into multiple groups with different speed limits.
- There could be potholes, traffic, and parking problems when driving.
Although they can occur, domestic flights are frequently less convenient than buses or railroads.
- Major cities are served by airlines including **Ryanair, easyJet, and ITA** Airways.
Cycling: There are bike paths all around Italy, some of which even accommodate electric bike options.
- Road cycling is very common in Northern Italy, especially in the Dolomites and Alps.
- Two websites that provide information on beaches and accessible facilities are **Village for All and Fondazione Cesare Serono.**

Websites and tools for reservations:
You'll discover everything you need for a smooth trip, from reliable lodging sites like **Booking.com, Plum Guide, Vrbo, and Airbnb** to necessary services like **Suntransfers** for airport transfers and **Trenitalia** for rail reservations. Learn insider advice on tour operators such as **Take Walks and Liv Tours** for unique experiences. Remember to download the suggested apps: **GetYourGuide, Viator, and Wanderlog** for browsing and booking tours and activities; **Omio or Skyscanner** for comparing and booking train, bus, and airline rates; and **Welcome Pickups** for airport

transfers. If you follow these crucial suggestions, your trip to Italy will be stress-free and unforgettable!

Travellers' Insurance:
For your vacation to Italy, we advise purchasing emergency medical insurance worth at least $50,000. **Medical Evacuation & Repatriation**: Pays for emergency transportation to a different hospital or, in the event that your treating physician determines that returning home is necessary for better care, to your country of origin.

Note that:
Petty theft is the major thing to watch out for when visiting Italy. Pickpocketing and bag snatching are two examples of these small-scale crimes that mostly happen in popular tourist destinations like Rome, Florence, and Venice.

Keep an eye out for valuables and leave pricey jewellery or watches at home. **Manners for Kissing a Cheek**: Italians frequently kiss one other on the cheek when mingling. Observe social cues; if you feel uncomfortable, a simple handshake will suffice.

Scan the QR code below and search for the Location you are going to in Italy and have a better view. Safe travels.

The map is the same on your phone. Consider taking screenshots as you walk around with no connection needed. Alternatively, you can contact the tourist office using the addresses and numbers provided in this guide.

In most cases, I use the Wanderlog site or app to plan my trip itinerary and expenses. You can try it if you're interested. Scan the QR code to learn more.

Transportation

Below are recommended Transportation related services in the city. It is advisable to make reservations online at the **Omio** site or by scanning the QR code.

Transport Services

Below are recommended transportation-related services in the city. Contact them if necessary upon landing at the nearby airport. It is advisable to make reservations online at the omio site or by scanning the QR code above.

- Taxi Chiavari:
 - Type: Taxi service
- Address: Stazione ferroviaria, Piazza Nostra Signora dell'Orto
- Phone: +39 0185 308284
- Provides taxi service in Chiavari, Italy, operating from the railway station area.

- Chiavari Toll Booth:
  - Type: Toll booth
  - Address: Salita al casella di
  - Open 24 hours for toll collection in Chiavari, Italy.

- Biglietteria Trenitalia Chiavari:
  - Type: Transportation service (Train ticket office)
  - Address: Piazza Nostra Signora dell'Orto, 19
  - Sells train tickets and provides information on train services in Chiavari.

- Giada Autonoleggio:
  - Type: Car rental agency
  - Address: Via Privata da Piazza Sanfront, 24
  - Phone: +39 0185 301420
  - Offers car rental services in Chiavari, Italy.

Accommodation

When travelling, it's advisable to book your hotel in advance.

Consider using bookings for great deals, available for registered hotels worldwide. Scan the QR code to book online. Here are some recommended hotels to consider:

- Hotel Dell'Orto Chiavari:
  - Location: Piazza Nostra Signora dell'Orto, 3
  - Phone: +39 0185 390448
  - Relaxed accommodation with an informal restaurant and bar, offering a mix of modern and classic rooms.

- Hotel Stella del Mare:
  - Location: Viale Enrico Millo, 115
  - Phone: +39 0185 322446

- Informal hotel featuring unfussy rooms, a restaurant, terrace, and complimentary Wi-Fi and breakfast for guests.

- Hotel Ferrari - Chiavari (GE):
  - Location: Corso De Michiel, 57
  - Phone: +39 0185 308604
  - Low-key hotel with a snack bar, free Wi-Fi, and breakfast, providing a comfortable stay for travellers.

- Albergo Santa Maria di Gilio Viana C. S. A. S.:
  - Location: Viale Tito Groppo, 29
  - Phone: +39 0185 363330
  - Casual property offering unpretentious rooms with some sea views, along with a restaurant and bright bar.

- Hotel Ristorante Zia Piera:
  - Location: Corso Valparaiso, 54
  - Phone: +39 0185 598047
  - Down-to-earth hotel providing breakfast, a sundeck, hot tub, pizzeria, and bar for a relaxing stay.

- Hotel San Pietro | Chiavari:
  - Location: Corso Valparaiso, 182
  - Phone: +39 0185 307672

- Modest waterfront lodging offering straightforward rooms, a casual restaurant, and bar for guests' convenience.

- Hotel Monte Rosa:
  - Location: Via Monsignor Luigi Marinetti, 6
  - Phone: +39 0185 300321
  - Laid-back hotel with a restaurant, two bars, outdoor pool, and breakfast, providing a comfortable retreat for travellers.

- Albergo Miramare:
  - Location: Corso Valparaiso, 56
  - Phone: +39 0185 309891

- Unassuming hotel opposite the beach, offering a free breakfast buffet and seafood restaurant for guests' enjoyment.

- Stella di Mare:
 - Location: Lavagna, Metropolitan City of Genoa, Italy
 - Phone: +39 0185 304462
 - Bright rooms with terraces, breakfast, bar, and sea views, providing a relaxed stay for visitors to Lavagna.

Restaurants

Try any of the top recommended restaurants known for their pleasant services, mouthwatering menus, and reasonable prices. You can reach them through the provided contact details.

- La Carraca:
  - Location: Via Entella, 50/52
  - Phone: +39 347 495 4130
- Traditional Ligurian restaurants offering specialties like Pesto Genovese, Focaccia, and Cima alla Genovese.

- Da Vittorio:
  - Location: Via Bighetti, 33
  - Phone: +39 0185 305093
  - Ligurian restaurants serving dishes such as Farinata, Acciughe al Verde, and Torta Pasqualina.

- Osteria Moderna:
  - Location: Via Vittorio Veneto, 7
  - Phone: +39 338 376 6675
  - Italian eatery offering classic dishes like Cappon Magro and Trofie al Pesto, prepared with fresh local ingredients.

- Da Felice:
  - Location: Corso Valparaiso, 136
  - Phone: +39 0185 308016
  - Seafood restaurant known for its specialties like Frittura di Pesce and Panigacci con Pecorino e Salumi.

- Cantina Reggiana:
  - Location: Via Giuseppe Raggio, 27
  - Phone: +39 0185 308338
  - Italian restaurant featuring dishes such as Cima alla Genovese and Farinata, prepared with care and expertise.

- Lord Nelson Pub Restaurant:

- Location: Corso Valparaiso, 27
- Phone: +39 0185 302595
- Seafood-focused eatery offering Ligurian classics like Acciughe al Verde and Trofie al Pesto, paired with local wines.

- La Stiva:
    - Location: 24 Via Porto Turistico, Corso Cristoforo Colombo
    - Phone: +39 0185 175 6919
    - Casual restaurants serving a variety of dishes including Pizza, Pasta, and Seafood, prepared with authentic Italian flavours.

- Luchin:
    - Location: Via Bighetti, 53
    - Phone: +39 0185 301063
    - Ligurian restaurant renowned for its Pesto Genovese, Farinata, and Acciughe al Verde, prepared according to traditional recipes.

Shopping

Below are recommendable shops in the city. Explore shopping in any of these stores and bring back some souvenirs.

- G & G:
  - Type: Shopping mall
  - Address: Via Jacopo Rocca, 50
  - Phone: +39 0185 363816
  - Offers a variety of products and services for shoppers, located at Via Jacopo Rocca, 50.

- Casa Shopping:
  - Type: Store
  - Address: Via Cesare Battisti, 26

- Phone: +39 0185 382310
- Provides a diverse range of items for purchase, situated at Via Cesare Battisti, 26.

- Golfo Tigullio Srl:
  - Type: Shopping mall
  - Address: Via Parma, 392
  - Phone: +39 0185 383300
  - Features a selection of shops and services, located at Via Parma, 392.

- Di Per Di srl:
  - Type: Shopping mall
  - Address: Via Martiri della Liberazione, 119
  - Phone: +39 0185 311724
  - Offers various retail options for customers, situated at Via Martiri della Liberazione, 119.

- Opportunity Shop Chiavari:
  - Type: Store
  - Address: Corso Dante, 87
  - Provides an array of items for sale, located at Corso Dante, 87.

- Beach Break Shop Chiavari:
  - Type: Clothing store
  - Address: Via dei Revello, 29
  - Phone: +39 0185 599489

- Offers a selection of clothing and accessories, situated at Via dei Revello, 29.

- Blauer Store Chiavari:
  - Type: Clothing store
  - Address: Piazza Roma, 2
  - Phone: +39 0185 598043
  - Provides a range of clothing options for shoppers, located at Piazza Roma, 2.

- Honey:
  - Type: Women's clothing store
  - Address: Via Martiri della Liberazione, 169
  - Phone: +39 0185 362819
  - Offers a variety of women's clothing items, situated at Via Martiri della Liberazione, 169.

Phrases and Slang Terms

Basic Italian phrases and area slang terms to be familiar with before travelling.

- Buongiorno (Good morning)
- Buonasera (Good evening)
- Ciao (Hello/Hi)
- Arrivederci (Goodbye)

- Grazie (Thank you)
- Prego (You're welcome)
- Per favore (Please)
- Scusi (Excuse me)
- Mi scusi (Excuse me, formal)
- Mi dispiace (I'm sorry)

- Posso avere...? (Can I have...?)
- Quanto costa? (How much does it cost?)
- Dove si trova...? (Where is...?)
- Parla inglese? (Do you speak English?)
- Non parlo italiano (I don't speak Italian)

- Mi chiamo... (My name is...)
- Come ti chiami? (What's your name?)
- Io sono... (I am...)
- Di dove sei? (Where are you from?)

- Sono di... (I am from...)
- Vorrei... (I would like...)
- Non capisco (I don't understand)
- Può aiutarmi? (Can you help me?)

- Dove si trova il bagno? (Where is the bathroom?)
- Posso pagare con carta di credito? (Can I pay by credit card?)
- Posso prendere un taxi? (Can I take a taxi?)
- Mi può consigliare un buon ristorante? (Can you recommend a good restaurant?)
- Mi potrebbe portare al...? (Could you take me to...?)
- A che ora chiude? (What time does it close?)

- A che ora apre? (What time does it open?)
- Mi potrebbe dare lo scontrino? (Could you give me the receipt?)
- Quanto tempo ci vuole per arrivare a...? (How long does it take to get to...?)
- Sto cercando un hotel. (I'm looking for a hotel.)

- Dove posso trovare un bancomat? (Where can I find an ATM?)
- Mi sento male. (I feel sick.)
- Ho bisogno di un medico. (I need a doctor.)
- Ho perso il mio passaporto. (I've lost my passport.)

- Ho bisogno di aiuto. (I need help.)
- Ho fame. (I'm hungry.)
- Ho sete. (I'm thirsty.)

- Posso avere l'acqua del rubinetto? (Can I have tap water?)
- Vorrei prenotare una tavola per due. (I'd like to book a table for two.)
- Mi piace molto questo posto. (I really like this place.)
- Posso avere un'altra birra, per favore? (Can I have another beer, please?)

- Questo cibo è delizioso. (This food is delicious.)
- Mi può dare il menu? (Can you give me the menu?)
- Posso avere del sale/pepe? (Can I have some salt/pepper?)
- È inclusa la mancia nel conto? (Is the tip included in the bill?)

- Vorrei fare una prenotazione. (I would like to make a reservation.)
- Posso avere un'altra coperta/cuscino? (Can I have another blanket/pillow?)
- Dove posso trovare il wifi gratuito? (Where can I find free wifi?)

- Mi può consigliare qualche posto da visitare? (Can you recommend some places to visit?)
- Mi potrebbe dare indicazioni per il centro città? (Could you give me directions to the city center?)

- Qual è il modo migliore per raggiungere la spiaggia? (What's the best way to get to the beach?)
- A che ora parte il treno per...? (What time does the train to... leave?)
- Quanti euro sono...? (How many euros are...?)
- Vorrei una camera singola/doppia. (I would like a single/double room.)

- Vorrei noleggiare una macchina. (I would like to rent a car.)
- Mi può chiamare un taxi? (Can you call me a taxi?)
- Quanto tempo ci vuole per arrivare all'aeroporto? (How long does it take to get to the airport?)
- Dove posso trovare un negozio di souvenir? (Where can I find a souvenir shop?)
- Vorrei cambiare dei soldi. (I would like to exchange some money.)

- Mi può consigliare un buon bar? (Can you recommend a good bar?)
- Questo è troppo caro. (This is too expensive.)
- Posso provare questo? (Can I try this on?)

- Dove posso trovare la fermata dell'autobus? (Where can I find the bus stop?)
- Mi potrebbe chiamare un'ambulanza? (Could you call an ambulance for me?)
- Sto cercando la farmacia più vicina. (I'm looking for the nearest pharmacy.)
- Vorrei una bottiglia d'acqua. (I would like a bottle of water.)

- Posso avere un gelato al cioccolato/vaniglia? (Can I have a chocolate/vanilla ice cream?)
- Questo treno va a...? (Does this train go to...?)
- A che ora parte l'autobus per...? (What time does the bus to... leave?)
- Vorrei visitare il museo. (I would like to visit the museum.)
- Mi potrebbe aiutare con i bagagli? (Could you help me with the luggage?)

- Posso pagare in contanti? (Can I pay in cash?)
- Dove posso trovare una lavanderia self-service? (Where can I find a self-service laundry?)
- Vorrei una mappa della città. (I would like a map of the city.)
- Dove posso noleggiare una bicicletta? (Where can I rent a bike?)
- Quanto costa un biglietto per...? (How much is a ticket to...?)

- Vorrei andare alla stazione ferroviaria. (I would like to go to the train station.)
- Vorrei prenotare un taxi per domani mattina. (I would like to book a taxi for tomorrow morning.)
- Mi potrebbe consigliare un buon libro da leggere? (Could you recommend a good book to read?)

- Posso avere il conto, per favore? (Can I have the bill, please?)
- Vorrei andare al centro commerciale. (I would like to go to the shopping center.)
- C'è un mercato nelle vicinanze? (Is there a market nearby?)
- Vorrei prenotare un tour della città. (I would like to book a city tour.)
- Mi piacerebbe fare una passeggiata in centro. (I would like to take a walk downtown.)

- Posso avere una mappa dei trasporti pubblici? (Can I have a map of public transportation?)
- Vorrei noleggiare un'auto per il weekend. (I would like to rent a car for the weekend.)
- Dove posso trovare il parcheggio più vicino? (Where can I find the nearest parking lot?)
- Mi potrebbe aiutare a trovare un hotel economico? (Could you help me find a budget hotel?)
- Vorrei una camera con vista sul mare. (I would like a room with a sea view.)

- Posso avere un'altra coperta, per favore? (Can I have another blanket, please?)
- Vorrei sapere se c'è una palestra nelle vicinanze. (I would like to know if there is a gym nearby.)
- Mi scusi, dove posso trovare un negozio di souvenir? (Excuse me, where can I find a souvenir shop?)

- Posso avere informazioni sul trasporto pubblico? (Can I have information about public transportation?)
- Mi potrebbe consigliare un buon posto per fare shopping? (Could you recommend a good place for shopping?)
- Come posso raggiungere il centro storico? (How can I reach the historical center?)

- Quali sono le attrazioni principali della città? (What are the main attractions of the city?)
- Vorrei prenotare un tour guidato. (I would like to book a guided tour.)
- Mi piacerebbe assaggiare piatti tipici della regione. (I would like to try typical dishes of the region.)
- C'è qualche evento o festività locale durante il mio soggiorno? (Is there any local event or festival during my stay?)

- Potrebbe consigliarmi un buon punto panoramico per scattare delle foto? (Could you recommend a good viewpoint for taking photos?)

- Dove posso trovare un ufficio turistico per ottenere informazioni? (Where can I find a tourist office to get information?)
- Vorrei prenotare un biglietto per uno spettacolo o un evento. (I would like to book a ticket for a show or an event.)
- Qual è il modo migliore per esplorare la città a piedi? (What is the best way to explore the city on foot?)

- Mi potrebbe aiutare a organizzare un'escursione nelle vicinanze? (Could you help me organize an excursion nearby?)
- Vorrei noleggiare una bicicletta per esplorare la zona. (I would like to rent a bike to explore the area.)

- Cosa dovrei sapere sulle tradizioni locali e sulla cultura? (What should I know about local traditions and culture?)
- Mi potrebbe consigliare un posto tranquillo per rilassarsi? (Could you recommend a quiet place to relax?)

- Sto cercando un buon ristorante con cucina vegetariana/vegana. (I'm looking for a good restaurant with vegetarian/vegan cuisine.)

- Mi piacerebbe partecipare a una degustazione di vini locali. (I would like to participate in a tasting of local wines.)
- Quali sono le migliori spiagge della zona? (What are the best beaches in the area?)
- Mi potrebbe aiutare a prenotare un'escursione in barca? (Could you help me book a boat excursion?)

- Vorrei visitare qualche mercato locale per fare acquisti. (I would like to visit some local markets for shopping.)
- Mi potrebbe consigliare un bel sentiero per fare trekking? (Could you recommend a nice trail for hiking?)
- Sto cercando un posto per praticare sport acquatici come il surf o il kayak. (I'm looking for a place for water sports like surfing or kayaking.)

- Potrebbe darmi informazioni su eventi culturali o mostre d'arte? (Could you give me information about cultural events or art exhibitions?)
- Vorrei fare un giro in barca per esplorare la costa. (I would like to take a boat trip to explore the coast.)

- Mi potrebbe suggerire un'attività divertente da fare in famiglia? (Could you suggest a fun activity for the family?)
- Quali sono le migliori aree per lo shopping di prodotti locali? (What are the best areas for shopping for local products?)

- Vorrei visitare qualche chiesa storica o luogo di culto della città. (I would like to visit some historical churches or places of worship in the city.)
- Potrebbe consigliarmi un buon posto per gustare il gelato artigianale? (Could you recommend a good place to enjoy artisanal ice cream?)
- Mi potrebbe indicare un bel percorso panoramico da fare in macchina? (Could you point me to a scenic drive route?)
- Quali sono le principali festività locali da non perdere? (What are the main local festivals not to be missed?)

- Sto cercando un posto per fare una passeggiata romantica al tramonto. (I'm looking for a place for a romantic sunset walk.)
- Vorrei partecipare a una lezione di cucina per imparare a preparare piatti italiani. (I would like to attend a cooking class to learn how to prepare Italian dishes.)

- Mi potrebbe consigliare un bel posto per fare birdwatching? (Could you recommend a nice place for birdwatching?)
- Quali sono i migliori ristoranti con cucina internazionale nella zona? (What are the best restaurants with international cuisine in the area?)

- Vorrei noleggiare una barca a vela per una giornata in mare. (I would like to rent a sailboat for a day at sea.)
- Potrebbe suggerirmi un bel posto per fare snorkeling? (Could you suggest a nice place for snorkeling?)
- Mi potrebbe aiutare a organizzare una visita in una cantina locale? (Could you help me organize a visit to a local winery?)
- Vorrei prenotare un'esperienza di immersione subacquea. (I would like to book a scuba diving experience.)

- Mi potrebbe dare qualche consiglio su cosa fare in caso di emergenza? (Could you give me some advice on what to do in case of emergency?)
- Sto cercando un bel posto per fare un picnic romantico. (I'm looking for a nice place for a romantic picnic.)
- Vorrei partecipare a una lezione di yoga all'aperto. (I would like to join an outdoor yoga class.)

- Potrebbe indicarmi un buon posto per osservare le stelle di notte? (Could you point me to a good place to stargaze at night?)
- Quali sono le migliori discoteche o locali notturni della città? (What are the best nightclubs or bars in the city?)
- Vorrei fare una passeggiata lungo il lungomare al chiaro di luna. (I would like to take a moonlit stroll along the promenade.)
- Mi potrebbe consigliare un buon posto per fare equitazione? (Could you recommend a good place for horseback riding?)

Slang Terms
- Mica male: Not bad
- Che palle: What a drag
- Dai!: Come on!
- Che casino: What a mess
- Figata: Cool, awesome

- Fare baldoria: To have a blast, to party
- Essere al verde: To be broke
- Figo: Cool, trendy
- Sbatti: Bummer
- Ciao bello/a: Hi handsome/beautiful
- Che figo!: How cool!
- Fare una capatina: To drop by, to pay a quick visit
- Andare a farsi una birretta: To go grab a beer

- Che schifo: How disgusting
- Aperitivo: To have an aperitif

- Fare tardi: To be late
- Non fare lo sfigato: Don't be a loser
- Prendere un giro: To take a walk around
- Sbronzarsi: To get drunk
- Mi raccomando: Take care, be careful
- Essere un cretino: To be a jerk
- Non fare il fannullone: Don't be lazy

- Fai il furbo: Don't try to be clever
- Avere le palle: To be brave
- Andare in giro: To go around, to hang out
- Stai fresco!: Forget it!
- Dare una mano: To lend a hand
- Fai schifo!: You suck!
- Avere le palle quadre: To be old-fashioned

- Dai, su!: Come on, cheer up!
- Fare il cazzone: To act foolishly
- Che sbatti!: What a hassle!
- Essere in gamba: To be smart, skilled
- Avere un chiodo fisso: To have an obsession
- Stare sul chi vive: To be on edge

- Fare il furbetto: To be a little sneak
- Andare in fumo: To go up in smoke

- Avere una fissa: To have a fixation
- Che coglione!: What an idiot!
- Essere in giro: To be out and about
- Fatti una risata: Have a laugh
- Che casino!: What a mess!

- Fare il giro: To take a walk, stroll around
- Dare una scorsa: To give a ride
- Fare il furbacchione: To act like a smart aleck
- Che cattiveria!: How mean!
- Prendere per il culo: To make fun of someone
- Fai schifo!: You're disgusting!

Long Slang Terms
- Dai, su! Fatti una risata e prendiamo un giro in giro per la città. (Come on, cheer up! Let's have a laugh and take a stroll around the city.)
- Andiamo a farsi una birretta al bar? (Shall we go grab a beer at the bar?)
- Non fare il furbetto, dai una mano e aiutami con queste borse. (Don't be a smart aleck, lend a hand and help me with these bags.)

- Che figata, questo posto è proprio figo! (How cool, this place is really awesome!)
- Stai fresco! Non ci penso neanche! (Forget it! I'm not even considering it!)

- Dai, su! Non essere un cretino, andiamo a fare baldoria stasera! (Come on, cheer up! Don't be a jerk, let's party tonight!)
- Prendiamo un giro in giro per il centro e poi facciamo un aperitivo. (Let's take a walk around downtown and then have an aperitif.)

- Non fare il fannullone, è ora di mettersi al lavoro! (Don't be lazy, it's time to get to work!)
- Mi raccomando, fai attenzione mentre attraversiamo la strada. (Take care, be careful while we cross the street.)
- Che schifo, questo ristorante è proprio sporco! (How disgusting, this restaurant is really dirty!)

Liguria

Welcome to Liguria, the region that is home to the Italian Riviera and a definite must-visit in Europe. After falling in love with this region of Italy during a city break to Genoa last summer, I have been going there for years. If you're looking for somewhere fresh to visit, it's a great alternative to the Amalfi Coast or Puglia.

Liguria's Location

A region on Italy's northwest coast, Liguria is sandwiched between Tuscany, Emilia-Romagna, and Piremont. The Ligurian Sea envelops the port town of Genoa, which serves as the region's capital.

Beautiful beaches, port towns, fishing villages, and crystal-clear water define the region. Green hills and valleys can be found inland, making them ideal for exploring and trekking.

The region is covered in vineyards and olive groves, which contribute to Italy's delicious cuisine.

Which season is ideal for travelling to Liguria?

The Ligurian Coast is best visited in the summer, as it is in most of the Mediterranean. I would advise travelling between June and September just outside of these busy times, as July and August in particular may get very hot and crowded. There will be fewer visitors in May and October, when pleasant, warm weather is expected with the possibility of sporadic showers of rain.

I wouldn't advise visiting this area in the winter because it can get rather stormy from November to March, and many of the hotels and restaurants are closed during this time. stormy in the winter.

Shoulder season, which runs from April to May, is a great time to visit Liguria if you want to take advantage of low hotel and airfare prices. Be prepared for all kinds of weather during this time of year!

Travel Tips

By air: There are numerous European flights from Genoa's respectable international airport. There are 1-2 daily flights available to London throughout the year. There are flights from Manchester to Liguria for people in the UK's north.

By train: I would advise using the well-connected rail system to travel between the towns and villages. With direct trains to Milan, Nice (in France), Rome, and numerous other major Italian towns, Genoa is the main terminus. You can reach the shore from Genoa, which is home to communities like Santa Margherita, La Spezia, Camogli, and the Cinque Terre settlements.

By car: There are a lot of great places in Italy for a road trip, if that's what you're looking for. As you travel along stunning coastal roads, past picture-perfect villages, across hills, and across mountains, roll down your windows and take in the warm breeze. The fastest route is the autostrada, which stretches from east to west and provides breathtaking views as well.

A few things to consider when visiting this area:

Open an Easy Parking account if you drive. Since this will enable you to adjust the parking period if you intend to stay somewhat longer.

Settle into private beach beds. The majority of the beach's excellent areas are private, despite the excellent facilities.

Take advantage of the free white parking bay if you find one. The blue lines are compensated. Yellow lines are intended only for loading and for handicapped users.

Dishes in Liguria

Focaccia Genoese: Its dough is unleavened, baked at a temperature of 520°F to 570°F, and it is no taller than 1 inch.

Focaccia di Recco: Cheese-filled, crunchy, and thin.

Farinata: a nutritious dish cooked with olive oil and chickpea flour.

Panissa: A tasty and easy fried chickpea polenta.

Trofie with pesto: A classic and delectable pasta dish with a rich Genoese pesto sauce.

Rabbit in the Ligurian style: delicate rabbit paired with pine nuts and olives.

Corzetti: Medallions of pasta imprinted with the family crest, typically served with walnut sauce.

Pansotti: Walnut sauce-covered stuffed pasta topped with wild greens.

Gobeletti di Rapallo: Quince jam-filled shortcrust pastry.

Reminiscent of Baci di Dama, Baci di Alassio are hazelnut and chocolate pastries filled with chocolate ganache.

Best locations in Liguria
The locations that are worth visiting are listed below. They are ranked according to the popular ones. Choose the one you can cover based on how long you have.

- Cinque Terre

To get to Cinque Terre, drive to the train station in La Spezia. The five villages that make up Cinque Terre are all reachable by train. All five villages are accessible with a daily pass. The beach at Monterosso is good. You have two options: travel the opposite route and see every village before arriving in Monterosso to enjoy the beach. We took a different approach, and it felt really good.

- Noli Noli

There are fantastic private beaches with immaculately clear water in this charming mediaeval town. There's a good length of beach. Thus, you may locate a quiet spot even during busy times of year. You can tour the town after relaxing on the beach. It features a café and a few specialty small shops. Your entire day will be over quickly.

- Pisa

It's time to take in the sights after a long day at the beach. Discovering the marvel that is the Leaning Tower of Pisa would be a wonderful place to start. You'll notice as you go to Pisa how the hills give way to the stunning Tuscan countryside. If your taste senses need a rest, a Mc Donald's is on the way.

- Ligure

The region's longest stretch of sandy beach is found near Finale Ligure. Every segment is essentially the same. There's no shortage of kid-friendly activities. Your children will adore it.

- Marina Diano

Diano Marina offers a fantastic nightlife that is ideal for families. plenty of eateries and cafeteria options. If you want to enjoy the evening, I would suggest spending the night here. The Hotel Metropole is an excellent choice if you intend to stay here. The motel offers free on-site parking. Additionally featured is a private beach. The beach amenities are excellent. All beach gear, including tubes and floating beds, is available for free.

Bon Voyage

Printed in Great Britain
by Amazon